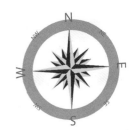

Explorers
Sticker Book

Illustrated by Paul Nicholls

Designed by Non Taylor

Written by Fiona Watt

Historical Consultant: Dr. Anne Millard

Contents

The Land of Punt 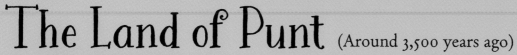 (Around 3,500 years ago)

Under the hot African sun, an Egyptian ship is being loaded with treasures. The expedition has been sent to the Land of Punt by Hatshepsut, Queen of Egypt, to encourage trading. The sailors are returning with jars of exotic spices, living frankincense trees, gold, animal skins and even wild animals.

Press on the stickers of the goods and the men loading the ship.

Viking voyages (in the year 1000)

After days and days of being tossed around on cold choppy seas, these hardy Vikings, including their leader, Leif Ericsson, have spotted a new land - North America. They set sail in search of new places to explore and settle, having heard sailors' tales of lands to the west of Greenland.

Fill the ship with the weary explorers. Add some inquisitive seagulls and some whales.

Leif Ericsson

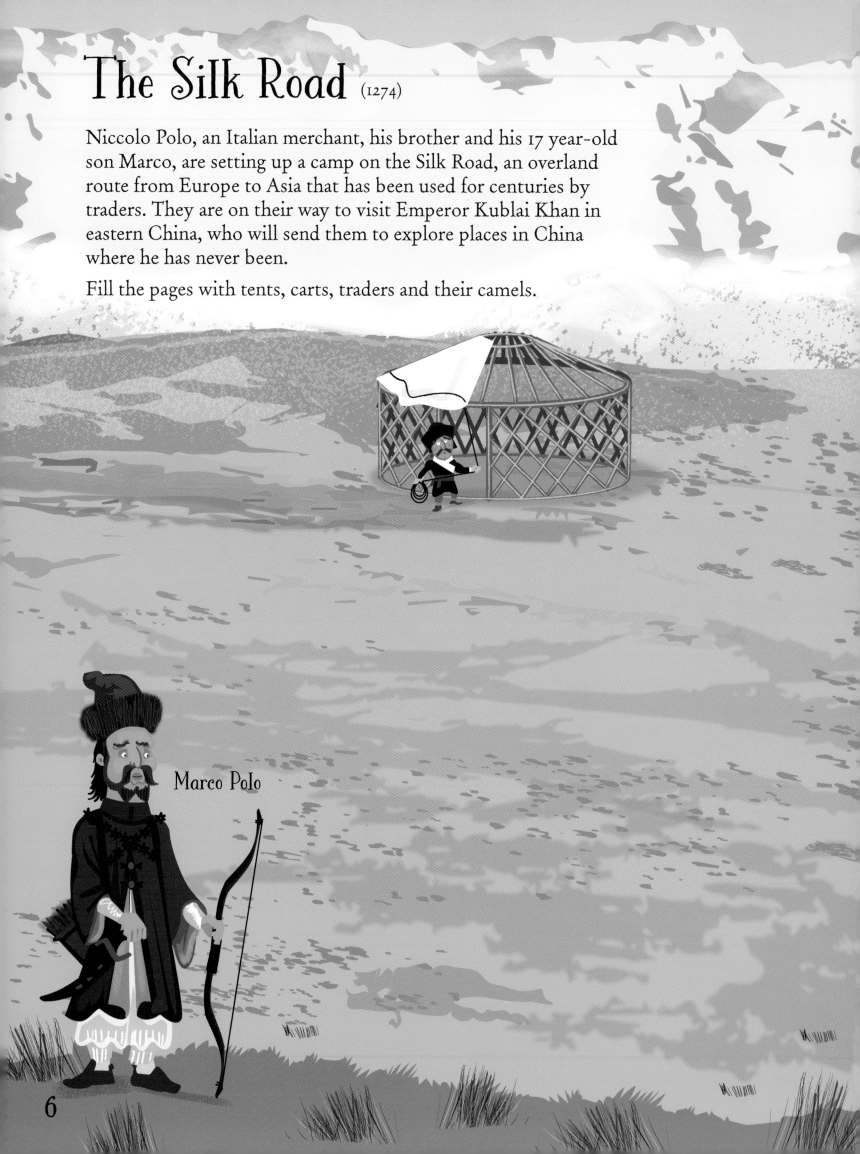

The Silk Road (1274)

Niccolo Polo, an Italian merchant, his brother and his 17 year-old son Marco, are setting up a camp on the Silk Road, an overland route from Europe to Asia that has been used for centuries by traders. They are on their way to visit Emperor Kublai Khan in eastern China, who will send them to explore places in China where he has never been.

Fill the pages with tents, carts, traders and their camels.

Marco Polo

The Treasure Fleet (1405)

Zheng He, a Chinese admiral, is standing on the deck of his ship, overseeing a fleet of over fifty ships. The Emperor has commanded the voyage to show the rest of the world how strong and powerful China is. Zheng He's mission is to explore the seas to the south and west of China, present gifts of gold, exotic silks and delicate porcelain to the rulers of places he visits, and to trade. The voyage will last almost two years and will take him around Southeast Asia and as far as India.

Use the stickers to create a fleet of ships sailing across the pages.

Zheng He

The Green Sea of Darkness (The Middle Ages)

In the 1450s, no one knew if it was possible to sail around Africa to reach the Indian Ocean. Sea captains found it hard to persuade their superstitious crews to sail south into the 'Green Sea of Darkness' to explore the lands beyond North Africa. Sailors had many fears about what they would find and whether they would ever return from a voyage.

Put the stickers of the sailors' fears and worries next to the descriptions.

Sailors believed the sea would get hotter and hotter the further south they sailed, until it boiled and set fire to their ship.

They thought that evil, gigantic sea monsters lurked beneath the waves, waiting to swallow a ship whole.

Some sailors believed that
the world was flat and if they
sailed too far from the coast,
they would fall over the edge.
Others feared ferocious storms
and enormous whirlpools.

They also thought
that beautiful
mermaids might lure
them down into the
watery depths where
they would drown.

A New World (1493)

Christopher Columbus is in the Spanish royal court, recounting tales of his latest expedition. He had tried to find a route to Asia by sailing west across the Atlantic Ocean. After a two-month voyage, his crew spotted land, but he hadn't reached Asia. He didn't know it, but he had landed in the West Indies, islands previously unknown to Europeans.

Press on the stickers of the King, Columbus and the courtiers. Add the goods, including native people and animals that he brought back from his voyage.

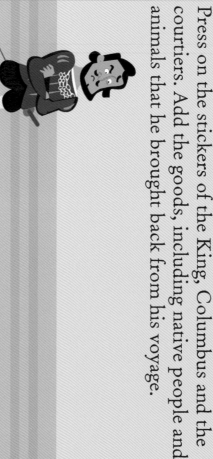

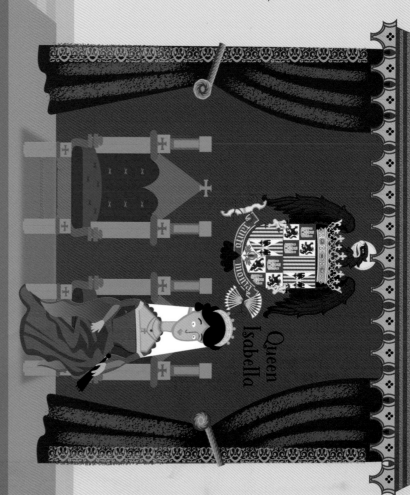

Queen Isabella

A passage to India (1498)

Vasco da Gama, a Portugeuse nobleman, is arriving in the Indian port of Calicut. He's had a long, sometimes treacherous, voyage around Africa into the Indian Ocean.

Fill the shore with sailors and the goods that they have brought to trade with the local king.

13

Around the world (1520)

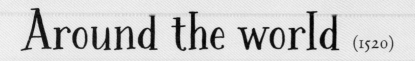

As a boy, Ferdinand Magellan had heard stories of Columbus's amazing voyages across the Atlantic Ocean. He's set off to search for a route across the ocean, around South America and then on to Asia. After several months at sea, Magellan and his men have discovered a waterway leading inland. They're unaware that this will lead lead them to the Pacific Ocean, across the Indian Ocean and back to Spain to complete the first voyage around the world.

Fill the ship with the crew going about their daily chores.

Ferdinand
Magellan

15

Grounded! (1770)

On their return voyage to England, after a scientific expedition to islands in the Pacific Ocean, disaster has struck. Captain James Cook and the crew of the *HMS Endeavour*, are frantically trying to remove the heavy cargo from their ship. It's stranded on a submerged coral reef that's punctured the hull. They're desperately hoping that they can refloat the ship by lightening its load.

Fill the beach with sailors and the heavy cargo.

Scientific exploration (1880)

As a young boy, Alexander von Humboldt was fascinated by nature. Now that he's an adult, he's set out on an expedition to South America, where he'll make scientific observations of rivers, mountains, volcanoes, jungles and the weather.

Use the stickers to fill the room with scientific instruments and samples that he's collected.

Alexander von Humboldt

Across America (1804)

After a gruelling journey along the Missouri River, explorers William Clark and Meriwether Lewis, along with their female guide and interpreter Sacagawea, are climbing a stony path, high in the Rocky Mountains. They are on a quest to find a route across America from St. Louis in the east, to the Pacific Ocean in the west.

Put the stickers of the weary explorers wending their way up the precipitous path.

Into the Outback (1860)

In the shade of a towering coolibah tree, a group of intrepid explorers are setting out to continue the final leg of their journey north across Australia. Little do they know, but the expedition will end in disaster, with neither of the expedition leaders, Robert Burke and William Wills, surviving the epic journey. Fill the campsite with tents and equipment, then add the fated explorers and their camels.

Exploring the Congo (1893)

Dressed in entirely unsuitable clothes for a journey through the humid African jungle, Mary Kingsley sits demurely on a trunk in the middle of a dugout canoe. She's on an expedition to study wildlife in the vast mangrove swamps of West Africa.

Put the sticker of Mary in the middle of the canoe, along with the people paddling. Add the wildlife, too.

To the South Pole (1911)

After two months of battling blizzards and perilous ice conditions, a team of exhausted explorers, led by Roald Amundsen, have arrived at the South Pole. They have erected a small tent and have proudly planted the Norwegian flag. Fill the ice with the members of the expedition. Then, add the weary huskies and the group's supplies.

22

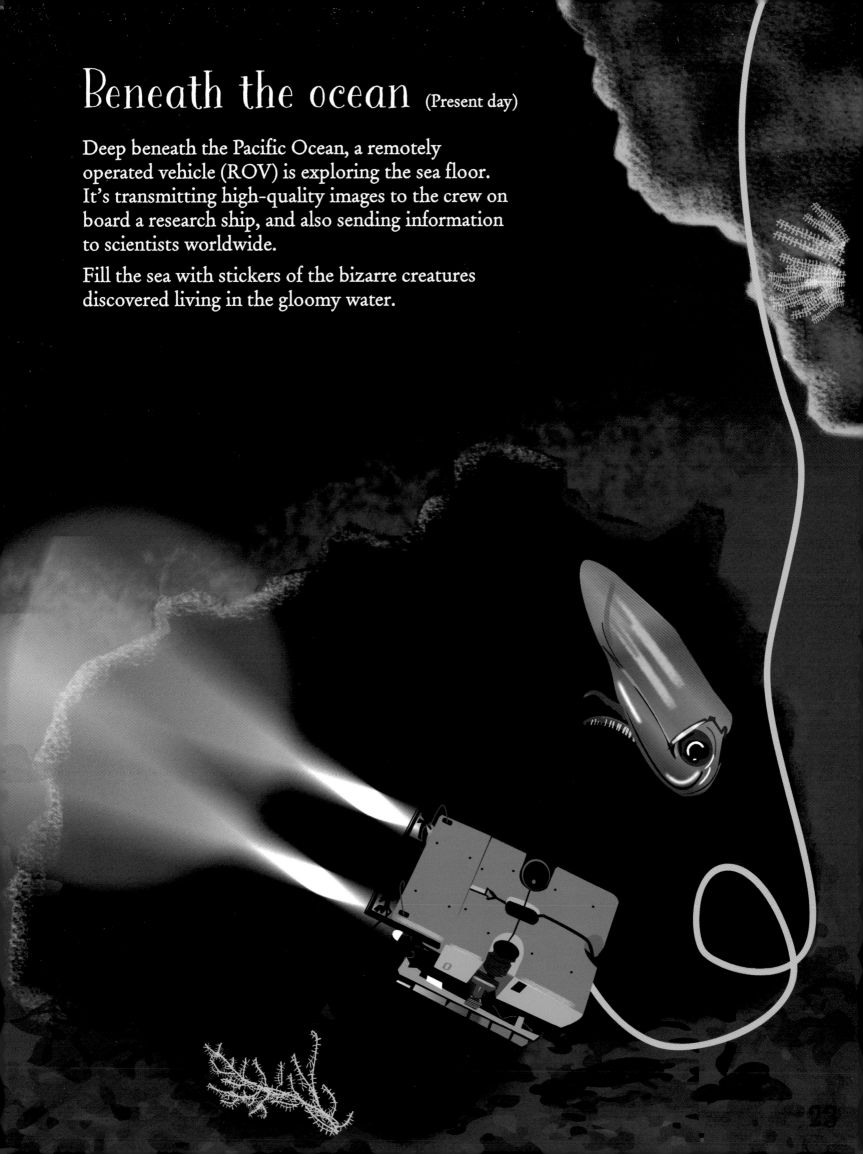

Beneath the ocean (Present day)

Deep beneath the Pacific Ocean, a remotely operated vehicle (ROV) is exploring the sea floor. It's transmitting high-quality images to the crew on board a research ship, and also sending information to scientists worldwide.

Fill the sea with stickers of the bizarre creatures discovered living in the gloomy water.

A map of the explorers' routes

Use the key to find out where the explorers went on their travels.

Key:
- Queen Hatshepsut
- Leif Ericsson
- Marco Polo
- Zheng He
- Christopher Columbus
- Vasco da Gama
- Ferdinand Magellan
- James Cook
- Alexander Von Humboldt
- Meriweather Lewis and William Clark
- Robert Burke and William Wills
- Mary Kingsley
- Roald Amundsen

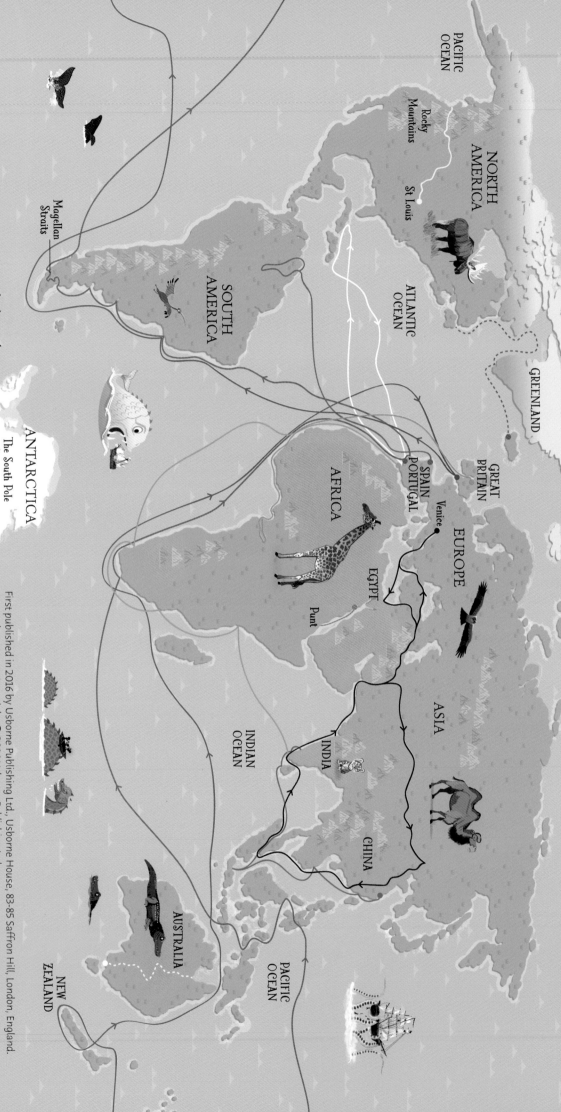

PACIFIC OCEAN

NORTH AMERICA

Rocky Mountains

St Louis

ATLANTIC OCEAN

GREENLAND

GREAT BRITAIN

SPAIN PORTUGAL

Venice

EUROPE

AFRICA

EGYPT

Punt

ASIA

INDIA

CHINA

SOUTH AMERICA

Magellan Straits

ANTARCTICA
The South Pole

Antarctica is not shown at its correct size or place on this map.

INDIAN OCEAN

AUSTRALIA

NEW ZEALAND

PACIFIC OCEAN

First published in 2016 by Usborne Publishing Ltd, Usborne House, 83-85 Saffron Hill, London, England. www.usborne.com Copyright © 2016 Usborne Publishing Ltd. The name Usborne and the devices ⓤ ⑂ are Trade Marks of Usborne Publishing Ltd.

24

The Land of Punt

Queen of Punt

King of Punt

Viking voyages

The Silk Road

The Treasure Fleet

A New World

Christopher Columbus

King Ferdinand of Spain

Page 12

A passage to India

Vasco da Gama

King of Calicut

Pages 13

Around the world

Pages 14-15

Grounded!

Captain James Cook

Pages 16-17